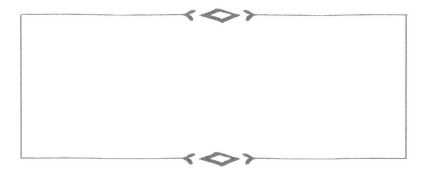

> True happiness is to enjoy the present without anxious dependence upon the future.
>
> – Seneca

This above all: to thine ownself be true.

— Shakespeare

> Excellence is not an act, but a habit.
>
> — Aristotle

> No act of kindness, no matter how small, is ever wasted.
> — Aesop

> The way to be happy is to make others so.
>
> – Robert Ingersoll

> We know what we are now, but
> not what we may become.
>
> – Shakespeare

> Do not take life too seriously -
> you will never get out of it alive.
>
> – Elbert Hubbard

> I am not bothered by the fact that I am not understood.
> — Confucius

> The greatest mistake you can make in life is to be continually fearing you will make one.
>
> – Elbert Hubbard

Made in the USA
Lexington, KY
17 July 2019